NITA FIRE AND CASUALTY COMPANY

v.

RUBINO AND SON, DRY CLEANERS

Problems and Case File

Anthony J. Bocchino
Louis M. Natali, Jr.

———————————

SECOND EDITION

THE NATIONAL INSTITUTE FOR TRIAL ADVOCACY

Address inquiries to:

Reprint Permission
National Institute for Trial Advocacy
1685 38th Street, Suite 200
Boulder, CO 80301-2735
Phone: (800) 225-6482
Fax: (720) 890-7069
Email: permissions@nita.org

ISBN 978-1-55681-065-7
FBNRU00

Printed in the United States of America

Official co-publisher of NITA.
WKLegaledu.com/NITA

<u>Nita Fire & Casualty Company</u>

v.

<u>Rubino and Son, Dry Cleaners</u>

<u>SUMMARY OF CONTENTS</u>

ACKNOWLEDGEMENTS

We express our appreciation to Professor James H. Seckinger, University of Notre Dame and Director of NITA, Jeffery V. Stuckey, Class of 1982, Notre Dame Law School, and John C. Greiner, Class of 1983, Notre Dame Law School, for their review and editing of this casefile. Their help was essential, and we are grateful.

We also thank Linda Kosinski and Nancy A. MacArthur for typing the manuscript, including the numerous revisions.

Finally, we note our appreciation to Dean Peter J. Liacouras, Temple University, for making the resources of the law school available to the authors and for his continuing support of the teaching of advocacy.

INTRODUCTION

The plaintiff, Nita Fire and Casualty Company, brought this lawsuit to recover an amount paid to the defendant, Anthony J. Rubino, on a fire insurance policy on Rubino's business. Rubino was doing business as Rubino and Son, Dry Cleaners.

A fire at the defendant's plant resulted in a total loss. The fire marshal determined that the fire was caused by spontaneous combustion. Relying on the report of the fire marshal, the plaintiff paid the defendant's claim in the amount of $300,000.00.

After paying the claim, the plaintiff learned from a former employee of the defendant that the fire possibly was caused by arson. After it conducted an independent investigation, the plaintiff decided that the fire was set deliberately. Rubino has denied the allegation of arson.

The setting for this case is Nita City, Nita. Nita City has a population of approximately two million people. It is a city of neighborhoods, each of which has its own name. One of the oldest neighborhoods is known as South Nita. The Rubino plant that was destroyed by fire was located in South Nita. The neighborhood had been undergoing a change of character during the decade prior to the fire, and it was in a declining economic state. Many small businesses had gone under, and the crime rate had increased dramatically. Many long-time residents were moving to more recently developed sections of the city.

One of these newer sections is known as the Northeast. It has been experiencing an economic boom for the past several years. It is considered a safe, middle-class section. Rubino built a new plant in the Northeast after the South Nita building was destroyed.

All years in these materials are stated in the following form:

> YR-0 indicates the actual year in which the case is being tried (i.e., the present year);
>
> YR-1 indicates the next preceding year (please use the actual year);
>
> YR-2 indicates the second preceding year (please use the actual year); etc.

PART ONE

RUBINO PROBLEMS

RUBINO PROBLEMS

TABLE OF CONTENTS

PROBLEMS

INTRODUCTION

The following problems are based on the <u>Nita Fire & Casualty Company v. Rubino and Son Dry Cleaners</u>, and they are intended to simulate realistic courtroom situations. Advance preparation is essential to their successful utilization as instructional materials. The materials within the Rubino case file must, of course, be mastered before attempting to perform the problems in a courtroom setting.

All years in these materials are stated in the following form:

<u>YR-0</u> indicates the actual year in which you are trying the case (i.e., the present year);

<u>YR-1</u> indicates the next preceding year (please use the actual year);

<u>YR-2</u> indicates the second preceding year (please use the actual year); etc.

Rubino Problems

A. Direct, Cross and Redirect Examination of Lay Witnesses.

PROBLEM 1

Raymond Rosen

Assume that the case is at trial and Raymond Rosen is the plaintiff's first witness.

- (a) On behalf of the plaintiff, prepare Mr. Rosen for trial.

- (b) On behalf of the plaintiff, conduct a direct examination of Mr. Rosen.

- (c) On behalf of the defendant, conduct a cross examination of Mr. Rosen.

- (d) On behalf of the plaintiff, conduct any necessary redirect examination.

PROBLEM 2

Edward George

Assume that the case is at trial and the plaintiff calls Edward George to testify.

- (a) On behalf of the plaintiff, prepare Mr. George for trial.

- (b) On behalf of the plaintiff, conduct a direct examination of Mr. George.

(c) On behalf of the defendant, conduct a cross examination of Mr. George.

(d) On behalf of the plaintiff conduct any necessary redirect examination.

PROBLEM 3

Anthony Rubino

Assume that Anthony Rubino is the defendant's first witness.

(a) On behalf of the defendant, prepare Mr. Rubino.

(b) On behalf of the defendant, conduct a direct examination of Anthony Rubino.

(c) On behalf of the plaintiff, conduct a cross examination of Anthony Rubino.

(d) On behalf of the defendant, conduct any necessary redirect examination.

PROBLEM 4

Robert Delgreggo

Assume that Anthony Rubino has already testified and that Delgreggo is the defendant's next witness.

(a) On behalf of the defendant prepare Mr. Delgreggo.

(b) On behalf of the defendant, conduct a direct examination of Robert Delgreggo.

(c) On behalf of the plaintiff, conduct a cross examination of Robert Delgreggo.

(d) On behalf of the defendant, conduct any necessary redirect examination.

B. **Exhibits and Demonstrative Aids.**

1. **Diagrams and Charts**

PROBLEM 5

Diagram of South Elm Street Plant

(a) On behalf of the plaintiff, examine Raymond Rosen and either introduce the diagram (case file page 45) as demonstrative evidence or use it as a demonstrative aid.

(b) On behalf of the defendant, oppose the introduction or use of the diagram and cross examine the witness.

2. **Writings**

PROBLEM 6

September 25 Letter

(a) On behalf of the plaintiff, introduce the letter from Edward George to Anthony Rubino dated September 25, YR-2 (case file page 47) by using a witness or witnesses of your choice.

(b) On behalf of the defendant oppose the offer.

PROBLEM 7

November 5 Letter

(a) On behalf of the plaintiff, introduce the claim letter, dated November 5, YR-2, (case file page 49) and the accompanying statement of loss (case file page 51) by using a witness or witnesses of your choice.

(b) For the defendant, oppose the offer.

PROBLEM 8

February 1 Letter and Check

(a) On behalf of the plaintiff, introduce the payment letter and check from the insurance company to Mr. Rubino, dated February 1, YR-1, (case file pages 53 and 55) by using a witness or witnesses of your choice.

(b) For the defendant, oppose the offer.

PROBLEM 9

February 15 Letter and February 1 Check

(a) On behalf of the defendant, introduce the correction letter from Anthony Rubino to the NITA Fire and Casualty Company, dated February 15, YR-1, (case file page 57) and the accompanying check, dated February 1, YR-1, (case file page 59) by using a witness or witnesses of your choice.

(b) On behalf of the plaintiff, oppose the offer.

PROBLEM 10

Joseph Ruggiero's Investigative Report

(a) On behalf of the defendant, introduce the investigative report, (case file page 63), by using a witness or witnesses of your choice.

(b) On behalf of the plaintiff, oppose the offer.

C. Impeachment and Rehabilitation.

PROBLEM 11

Raymond Rosen

Assume that the case is at trial and that the direct examination of Raymond Rosen has just been completed. Assume that during his direct examination Mr. Rosen testified that Anthony Rubino never offered him a job at the Northeast plant. In addition, the direct examination did not elicit the fact that Rosen stands to receive a reward if NITA Fire and Casualty Company prevails.

(a) On behalf of the defendant conduct a cross examination of Mr. Rosen on an issue or issues presented above.

(b) On behalf of the plaintiff conduct any necessary redirect examination.

PROBLEM 12

Anthony Rubino

For the purposes of this problem you may utilize the following excerpts from Anthony Rubino's direct examination at trial and his pre-trial deposition (case file page 21).

Direct Examination of Anthony Rubino
by Plaintiff's Trial Counsel [Excerpt
of Trial Testimony]:

*   *   *

When I arrived at the fire I spoke with Joe Ruggiero, the Fire Marshal. He asked me if there was any reason I knew why someone would want to set fire to the plant. I told him no. Then he asked me if any of my employees had a criminal record, and I mentioned that Bobby Delgreggo had had some trouble with the law in the past.

In addition, assume that on direct examination Anthony Rubino essentially repeats the explanation found in his letter to NITA Fire and Casualty Company regarding the $6,000 claim for lost uniforms. Refer to Rubino's deposition at page 21 of the case file.

(a) For the plaintiff, conduct a cross examination of Mr. Rubino on an issue or issues presented above.

(b) For the defendant, conduct any necessary redirect examination.

PROBLEM 13

Robert Delgreggo

Assume for the purpose of this problem that the direct examination of Bobby Delgreggo has just been completed. The direct examination did not elicit the fact that Delgreggo had been previously convicted of arson.

(a) For the plaintiff, conduct a cross examination of Mr. Delgreggo.

(b) For the defendant, conduct any necessary redirect examination.

D. **Adverse Examination.**

PROBLEM 14

Anthony Rubino

Assume that Anthony Rubino has been called adversely by the plaintiff.

   (a) On behalf of the plaintiff, conduct an adverse examination of Mr. Rubino on whatever topics you deem appropriate.

   (b) On behalf of the defendant, examine Mr. Rubino without calling him as your own witness.

PROBLEM 15

Raymond Rosen

Assume that Raymond Rosen has demonstrated hostility towards defense's lawyer during deposition.

   (a) On behalf of the defendant, conduct an adverse examination of Mr. Rosen on whatever topics you deem appropriate.

   (b) On behalf of the plaintiff examine Mr. Rosen without calling him as your own witness.

E. <u>Discovery Depositions</u>.

PROBLEM 16

Edward George

(a) On behalf of the defendant, take a discovery deposition of Edward George.

(b) On behalf of the plaintiff, represent your client's interests at the deposition.

PROBLEM 17

Raymond Rosen

(a) On behalf of the defendant, take a discovery deposition of Raymond Rosen.

(b) On behalf of the plaintiff, represent your client's interests at the deposition.

PROBLEM 18

Bryce Pugh

(a) On behalf of the defendant, take a discovery deposition of Bryce Pugh.

(b) On behalf of the plaintiff, represent your client's interests at the deposition.

PROBLEM 19

Robert Delgreggo

(a) On behalf of the plaintiff, take a discovery deposition of Robert Delgreggo.

(b) On behalf of the defendant, represent your client's interests at the deposition.

PROBLEM 20

Joseph Ruggiero

(a) On behalf of the plaintiff, take a discovery deposition of Joseph Ruggiero.

(b) On behalf of the defendant, represent your client's interests at the deposition.

PROBLEM 21

Anthony Rubino

(a) On behalf of the plaintiff, take a discovery deposition of Anthony Rubino.

(b) On behalf of the defendant, represent Anthony Rubino at the deposition.

F. Examination of Expert Witnesses.

PROBLEM 22

Bryce Stenton Pugh

Assume that the plaintiff has called Bryce Stenton Pugh as a witness.

 (a) On behalf of the plaintiff, conduct a direct examination of Mr. Pugh.

 (b) On behalf of the defendant, conduct a cross examination of Mr. Pugh.

 (c) On behalf of the plaintiff, conduct any necessary redirect examination.

PROBLEM 23

Joseph Ruggiero

Assume that the defendant has called Joseph Ruggiero as a witness.

 (a) On behalf of the defendant, conduct a direct examination of Mr. Ruggiero.

 (b) On behalf of the plaintiff, conduct a cross examination of Mr. Ruggiero.

 (c) On behalf of the defendant, conduct any necessary redirect examination.

G. Jury Selection.

PROBLEM 24

Due to time constraints, only four jurors will be selected. Each party will be limited to one peremptory challenge. Use the jury information sheet that follows this problem.

(a) On behalf of the plaintiff, conduct a <u>voir dire</u> and select a jury.

(b) On behalf of the defendant, conduct a <u>voir dire</u> and select a jury.

JURY INFORMATION SHEET

    Please assume the role of a person whom you know well, so you will be able to answer <u>voir dire</u> questions in that role. Please be realistic. Try to pick a role that would be commonly represented on a jury panel <u>and not a role of an eccentric</u>. By taking an eccentric role, you would impair the realism and benefit of the exercise for your fellow students both those who serve as counsel and those who observe the exercise.

    Please fill in the following form and be prepared to use it at the session on Problem 30. You may be asked to deliver it to the instructor in advance of or during the session.

Your real name: _____

Information About You in Your Assumed Role

1. Name: _____

2. Age: _____

3. Address in NITA City: _____

    Characterize the neighborhood: _____

    _____

4. Length of residence in NITA City: _____

5. Occupation: _____

    Duties in that occupation: _____

    _____

6. Marital Status: _____

7. Number and ages of children: _____

8. Number of years of education: _____

9. Other relevant information: _____

    _____

    _____

Rubino Problems

H. Opening Statements.

PROBLEM 25

Each participant will have approximately seven to ten minutes to present an opening statement.

     (a) On behalf of the plaintiff, give an opening statement.

     (b) On behalf of the defendant, give an opening statement.

I. Closing Arguments.

PROBLEM 26

Each participant will have approximately ten to twelve minutes to present a closing argument. Because that may be insufficient time for a complete closing argument, be prepared to indicate what further topics you would have covered if time had permitted.

Assume that all available witnesses have testified in accordance with their prior statements or depositions and that all exhibits contained in the case file have been introduced into evidence.

     (a) On behalf of the plaintiff, give a closing argument.

     (b) On behalf of the defendant, give a closing argument.

Rubino Problems

PART TWO

RUBINO CASE FILE

RUBINO CASE FILE

TABLE OF CONTENTS

INTRODUCTION

The plaintiff, Nita Fire and Casualty Company, brought this lawsuit to recover an amount paid to the defendant, Anthony J. Rubino, on a fire insurance policy on Rubino's business. Rubino was doing business as Rubino and Son, Dry Cleaners.

A fire at the defendant's plant resulted in a total loss. The fire marshal determined that the fire was caused by spontaneous combustion. Relying on the report of the fire marshal, the plaintiff paid the defendant's claim in the amount of $300,000.00.

After paying the claim, the plaintiff learned from a former employee of the defendant that the fire possibly was caused by arson. After it conducted an independent investigation, the plaintiff decided that the fire was set deliberately. Rubino has denied the allegation of arson.

The setting for this case is Nita City, Nita. Nita City has a population of approximately two million people. It is a city of neighborhoods, each of which has its own name. One of the oldest neighborhoods is known as South Nita. The Rubino plant that was destroyed by fire was located in South Nita. The neighborhood had been undergoing a change of character during the decade prior to the fire, and it was in a declining economic state. Many small businesses had gone under, and the crime rate had increased dramatically. Many long-time residents were moving to more recently developed sections of the city.

One of these newer sections is known as the Northeast. It has been experiencing an economic boom for the past several years. It is considered a safe, middle-class section. Rubino built a new plant in the Northeast after the South Nita building was destroyed.

All years in these materials are stated in the following form:

> YR-0 indicates the actual year in which the case is being tried (i.e., the present year);
>
> YR-1 indicates the next preceding year (please use the actual year);
>
> YR-2 indicates the second preceding year (please use the actual year); etc.

SPECIAL INSTRUCTIONS FOR USE AS A FULL TRIAL

When this case file is used as the basis of a full trial, the following witnesses may be called by the parties:

Plaintiff: Raymond Rosen — retired store manager — used to be accounting
              Edward George - accountant
              Bryce Stenton Pugh insurance investigator

Defendant: Anthony Rubino
              Robert Delgreggo - works @ plant
              Joseph Ruggiero Fire Marshall

A party need not call all of the persons listed as its witnesses. Any or all of the witnesses can be called by either party. However, if a witness is to be called by a party other than the one for whom he is listed, the party for whom the witness is listed will select and prepare the witness.

The parties have agreed to the following stipulations:

(1) The signatures on all documents are authentic.

(2) The fire insurance policy on 1050 South Elm Street, Nita City, Nita, was in force on October, YR-2.

(3) The $300,000 claim by the insured, Rubino and Son, Dry Cleaners, was paid in full on February, YR-1 after being adjusted by Nita Fire and Casualty Company.

(4) The diagram of 1050 South Elm Street is a reasonable representation of the Rubino plant as it existed on October 28, YR-2. It is not drawn to scale, however, and may be used only for illustration purposes.

(5) John Andrews is unavailable to testify as a witness. The parties have agreed to the facts attributed to Andrews in the report of the fire marshal, Joseph Ruggiero.

(6) The claim letter and claim form following the Rubino deposition are business records of Nita Fire and Casualty Company.

(7) There is no accountant-client privilege in the state of Nita.

A. PLEADINGS.

IN THE CIRCUIT COURT OF
DARROW COUNTY, NITA
CIVIL DIVISION

NITA FIRE AND CASUALTY COMPANY,	)	
	)	
Plaintiff,	)	
	)	
v.	)	COMPLAINT
	)	
ANTHONY J. RUBINO, D.B.A.	)	
RUBINO AND SON, DRY CLEANERS,	)	
	)	
Defendant	)	

The plaintiff for its claim against the defendant alleges:

1. At all times herein mentioned, the defendant, Anthony J. Rubino, d.b.a. Rubino and Son, Dry Cleaners, was and is a resident of the state of Nita and is doing business in the state of Nita.

2. On or about October 28, YR-2, the defendant's principal place of business was 1050 South Elm Street, Nita City, Nita.

3. At the present time, the defendant's principal place of business is 65100 Roosevelt Boulevard, Nita City, Nita.

4. At all times herein mentioned, the defendant was in the dry cleaning, laundry, and uniform rental business.

5. At all times herein mentioned, the plaintiff, Nita Fire and Casualty Company, was and is a Nita corporation, having its principal place of business at Number One Charter Oak Plaza in the city of Nita and the state of Nita.

6. At all times herein mentioned, the plaintiff was in the business of providing fire, accident, homeowners, business, and life insurance.

7. On or about March 1, YR-2, the plaintiff and the defendant entered into a contract for insurance, Policy No. BF-24-076-1112-5, providing <u>inter alia</u>:

Coverage

   (a) For coverage by the plaintiff in any amount up to and including $350,000.00 for any loss incurred by the defendant at his premises at 1050 South Elm Street, Nita City, Nita due to fire.

   (b) Provided, however, that there would be no payment by the plaintiff to the defendant for any loss due to fire caused as a result of the intentional actions of either the defendant or one acting in concert with the defendant.

8. On or about October 28, YR-2, the policy described in paragraph 7 was in force.

9. On or about October 28, YR-2, a fire occured at the premises at 1050 South Elm Street, Nita City, Nita.

10. On or about November 5, YR-2, the defendant made a claim for loss due to fire at the premises located at 1050 South Elm Street, Nita City, Nita, in the amount of $300,000.00 on Policy No. BF-24-076-1112-5.

11. On or about February 1, YR-1, the plaintiff paid the claim of the defendant on Policy No. BF-24-076-1112-5 in the amount of $300,000.00.

12. On or about February 15, YR-1, the defendant remitted to the plaintiff $6,000.00 due to a false statement made by the defendant in the defendant's claim of November 5, YR-2 on Policy No. BF-24-076-1112-5.

13. The fire that occurred on or about October 28, YR-2 at the premises located at 1050 South Elm Street, Nita City, Nita, was the result of intentional actions of the defendant or one acting in concert with the defendant, to wit: arson.

WHEREFORE, the plaintiff prays for judgement against the defendant in the amount of $294,000.00 in damages, together with interest as provided by law, the costs of this action, and such other and further relief as is just and proper.

JURY DEMAND

The plaintiff demands a trial by jury in this action.

THE PLAINTIFF

BY: *Linda L Shafer*

Linda L. Shafer
Shafer, Zinns and Klein
Public Ledger Bldg., 10th Fl.
Nita City, Nita

Dated: July 7, YR-1

RETURN OF SUMMONS

I hereby certify that the above complaint was personally served on Anthony Rubino on July 8, YR-1.

Wally Dee

Wally Dee
Process Server

IN THE CIRCUIT COURT OF
DARROW COUNTY, NITA
CIVIL DIVISION

NITA FIRE AND CASUALTY COMPANY,	)	
	)	
Plaintiff,	)	
	)	
v.	)	ANSWER
	)	
ANTHONY J. RUBINO, D.B.A.	)	
RUBINO AND SON, DRY CLEANERS,	)	
	)	
Defendant.	)	

Defendant, Anthony J. Rubino, for his answer to the plaintiff's complaint states:

1. Paragraphs 1, 2, 3, 4, 5, 6, 7, 8, 9, 10, and 11 are admitted.

2. Paragraphs 12 and 13 are denied.

WHEREFORE, the defendant moves to dismiss the claim of the plaintiff.

THE DEFENDANT

BY: *Carol Di Battiste*
Carol DiBattiste
DiBattiste, Cedrone and
   Difinuis
1492 Columbus Blvd.
Nita City, Nita

Dated: July 26, YR-1

B.   **Witnesses.**

The following pages contain depositions by various witnesses who will be available to testify at trial.

DEPOSITION OF RAYMOND ROSEN*

RAYMOND ROSEN, called to testify on deposition by the defendant and having been duly sworn, testified as follows:

My name is Ray Rosen. I am sixty-five years old. I'm retired now, but I used to be the supervisor and general manager of the Rubino and Son, Dry Cleaners, at 1050 South Elm Street in Nita City. I've lived at 1225 Catherine Street in South Nita for forty-five years. That's about three and a half blocks from where Rubino's used to be. I married my wife Louise in YR-40. We have two children. My married daughter lives in the Northeast section of Nita City and my son lives in Newtown.

I retired from Rubino's in February, YR-1 after thirty-six years of working for Mr. Rubino and after five years of working for his son, Tony. I was sorry I had to retire. I wasn't ready for it, but Tony wanted me to, and Mr. Rubino saw to it that I got a nice pension. Between the pension and my Social Security, we live okay. I had planned to retire when I was sixty-five, but I didn't want to help the kid, that is, Tony, set up the new plant in the Northeast anyway. I'd have done anything for Mr. Rubino, but not the kid.

My first job was with the old Nita Tool and Machine factory. When the factory moved to Newtown in YR-42, I took a job as a presser in the Rubino Dry Cleaners.

I always liked my job or at least I really liked working for Mr. Rubino. After a year or so working as a presser, I started doing other things. Soon I worked the counter, ordered supplies, did the bank deposits and payroll, and I did the regular maintenance on the machines. Mr. Rubino would always brag to the customers how I could fix almost anything with a paper clip and chewing gum.

Those were the good old days. Then Tony came out of the Navy and started working at the store. That was around YR-16. I guess the kid has a good head for business, but everything changed when Tony joined the business. Even the name of the place was changed to Rubino and Son.

---

*The transcript of Rosen's deposition was excerpted so that only his answers are reprinted here. Assume that this is a true and accurate rendering of those answers. This deposition was taken in the office of defendant's counsel on October 7, YR-1.

We started doing laundry in addition to dry cleaning. I used to know all the customers personally, but soon everyone became just a ticket number.

In YR-5, Mr. Rubino had a heart attack, and he had to retire. The store really changed then. We were doing more and more uniforms in the uniform rental business, but the machines were getting old and couldn't take the added loads. The machines were breaking down often. I had trouble putting them back together. Even the clothes rack was going. It skipped all the time, and it made a racket. Tony was involved with the branch stores that he had started in the Northeast. He told me that he wanted to put the money into the new stores and not into the South Nita store. I couldn't even persuade him to hire painters. I remember that, about a month or so before the fire, the customer area was looking so bad that Bobby Delgreggo and I went in on a Sunday and painted it ourselves.

Around YR-4, Tony brought in that fancy accountant. I think his name was Mr. George. He went through my books, did some kind of study of the neighborhood, and just went poking around the store. The accountant then talked to Tony about something called cost efficiency. Soon after, Tony told me that he and the accountant had agreed that they weren't going to put any more money into the South Elm Street store because the neighborhood was getting bad, and because the growth was in the Northeast. This happened around the time that we started doing uniforms.

I admit that South Nita isn't like it use to be, but all it needs is a little law and order. Like the day those crazy people took over Cohen's Department Store. A couple of people were killed, and a lot of others were hurt. Cohen's was just down the street from Rubino's. It had to close down because people were afraid to shop there.

Tony was real mad about that. I know that's one of the reasons why Tony decided to burn the store down--that and to get money for the new plant he wanted to open in the Northeast. A lot of times, I heard Tony and the accountant talking about the warehouse, and about how to get the money for it. That's why the accountant went over the store--to see where we could save money.

I heard Tony tell Bobby Delgreggo about the new warehouse, too. I thought Bobby was a nice kid. I knew he'd been in trouble before--and for arson too--but I thought that was all over. In fact, like I said earlier, he even went in on a Sunday about a month before the fire to help paint the customer area. I remember that I got a pain in my

fixed old machines

Bobby helped Paint - Why learn?

back, and he insisted I go home while he cleaned up all by himself. I know that he says the drop cloths and rags from that job were in the storage room. I can't say they weren't there but I didn't see them.

It was a couple days after the killings at Cohen's when I heard Bobby and Tony talking in the office. I was in the customer area going through the racks. I do that about once a week to take out orders that have been there for thirty days. I had my back to the office door, which was open. The diagram you showed me sets the store out pretty well. I heard Tony say, "We've got to get out of here." Then Bobby said, "Don't worry, I can take care of it." *no context*

Just then one of the pressers called to me, and I went into the work area. As soon as I was done, I went back to the racks. I heard Bobby say that he'd "get the money for the new warehouse." Tony said that he would "think about it."

It was about a week later that the place was burned down. You know, the fire destroyed everything. The only thing that was saved was the old safe. We opened it up, and everything inside was unburned. I noticed at that time, but really didn't think much of it then, that there was only a couple hundred dollars in the safe. Usually there'd be $2,000 to $3,000 there. *the safe*

The day before the fire, Tony did something real unusual. He ordered all the uniforms loaded into the trucks for the next day's delivery. We hardly ever load the day before delivery. Usually the trucks are loaded the same day. He also used all three trucks, when one truck would have been enough. Then he told the drivers to take the trucks to the Northeast stores that day. At the time, I couldn't understand why Tony would order the trucks out to the Northeast in the afternoon when deliveries are always made early in the morning. *Unusual behavior day before*

Well, around 5:00 the next morning, October 28th, YR-2, I get a call from Tony who told me to get to the store. Tony said that the store was on fire. I was the first one there, except for the Fire Department. Bobby got there next, then Tony. The place was in blazes by the time I got there. The fire chief or fire marshal asked Tony if any chemicals were kept in the plant. Tony told him the solvents were kept in the work area, and that Bobby kept the oil and tools for the trucks in the storage room. The marshal said that it looked like the fire started back there. He talked to me for a couple of minutes. I remember telling him about the layout of the store. When he asked, I told him that Bobby had been convicted for arson. *Chemicals in store*

-15-
Rubino Case File

Just then another hose was drawn in, and I had to move out of the way. I saw Bobby and Tony talking. I went over to where they were standing. Bobby looked real upset. Tony told Bobby not to worry. Tony said Bobby had been real good to him, and that Tony would take care of Bobby for the rest of his life.

A few months after the fire, in February YR-1, I met with Tony at one of the Northeast stores. Tony told me that he was going to open the new plant soon, and that there was a place for me there if I wanted it. I decided not to go with him, and he told me that I could retire if I wanted to. Like I said before, Mr. Rubino saw to it that I got my pension, so I didn't really have to keep working after the South Elm Street store was gone. As I was leaving the Northeast store, I passed Bobby in the parking lot. He was driving a brand new Cadillac. I wondered at the time where he got the money.

money for car could have come from anywhere

On my way home I started thinking. Everything started to add up--the conversation I overheard while at the racks, the new warehouse, Bobby being taken care of, his new Cadillac, the little amount of money in the safe, the trucks, the insurance. I thought about it for a couple more days, and then I went to the Fire Department.

thought about it for a few days

On February 15, YR-1, I told the fire marshal, Mr Ruggiero, that Bobby set the fire so that Tony could get the insurance money and buy the warehouse. He told me that I was nuts, and that he knew his business. He told me to get out, that the case was closed.

I went the next day to Al Case, the insurance agent. He put me in touch with the insurance company. I told the people there, at the Nita Fire and Casualty Company, everything that I've told you. They told me there was a ten percent reward for finding arsonists on policies they pay out on. This was after I told them what happened, so it didn't have anything to do with what I said.

(This deposition was taken in the office of defendant's counsel on October 7, YR-1. After it was transcribed, it was signed by the deponent, Raymond Rosen.)

Certified by:

Anne Dolan

ANNE DOLAN
Certified Shorthand Reporter (CSR)

DEPOSITION OF EDWARD GEORGE*

EDWARD GEORGE, called to testify on deposition by the defendant and having been duly sworn, testified as follows:

My name is Edward George. I am a member of Bryant, George and White, Certified Public Accountants and Business Consultants. I've been a member of this firm for twenty years.

I have a bachelor of science degree from Nita City University, and a master in business administration from Newtown State. I was certified as a public accountant in YR-18.

We have had an account with Anthony Rubino of Rubino and Son, Dry Cleaners, since YR-4. The account is for $5,000 per year. Our firm does the year-end accounting for Rubino's, and we give general planning advice. We also do their taxes.

I have personally advised Tony Rubino in his business affairs. This is not unusual. My associates and I agree that we are selling trust, and that it's important that we deal personally with our clients.

Mr. Rubino initially contacted our firm because he wanted advice on whether he should expand and renovate his Nita City dry cleaning plant and store at 1050 South Elm Street in Nita City. My people conducted a study of the neighborhood. The study included such factors as population growth, business pattern movement in the central business district, crime statistics, and average income, and the study revealed that the southern section of Nita City was in economic decline. I also examined the physical state of the facility and the records of the business for the period YR-9 through YR-5. I advised Mr. Rubino that I had concluded that, although his business was not showing a loss, it was not showing a reasonable profit. Although he had the money to make the necessary improvements on the South Nita facility, it would take him about five to eight years to retrieve his capital, and, still, he would not be guaranteed a profit or an expansion capability. I also updated his

study on Nita

5-8 yrs to regain what he put into

---

*The transcript of George's deposition was excerpted so that only his answers are reprinted here. Assume that this is a true and accurate rendering of those answers. This deposition was taken in the office of defendant's counsel on October 7, YR-1.

Explanation of less cash in the safe

accounting procedures. Mr. Rubino told me he was accustomed to keeping large amounts of money on hand. I instructed him not to do this, and to put that money in the bank. I also got him to put his records on a small home computer, and to accept charge cards.

I advised him to take as much money as he could squeeze out of the South Nita facility, and to invest it in the uniform rental business. I showed him exactly where he could cut corners, and I made some preliminary contacts with companies that used regular uniform service.

I explained to Mr. Rubino that the uniform business is a good companion to the regular laundry and dry cleaning business. The addition would require minimal cost, and his existing South Street facility would easily accommodate the added business for at least two to three years.

I knew Mr. Rubino did not want to move the South Street plant for personal reasons, but I did convince him to open a total of three retail outlets in the Northeast section of Nita City. The Northeast provides the fastest growing potential in the Nita City area. I was able to locate companies that would use the Rubino uniform service in this area.

Within three years, ninety percent of the Rubino business was located in the Northeast. I constantly told Mr. Rubino that he was losing money maintaining the South Street facility as the central plant, but he wanted it there because of his father, who had started the business. Mr. Rubino did agree that it was a good idea for me to look for a new facility in the Northeast large enough to handle the business from the three Northeast cleaning stores, the uniform business, and expansion. We also agreed that we would make plans to phase out the South Street facility.

Sept. 2020

In September, YR-2, I located a warehouse for sale at 65100 Roosevelt Boulevard in Northeast Nita City. I told Mr. Rubino about the warehouse, and we obtained an option to purchase. The letter you showed me is the copy of the original I sent to Mr. Rubino, and it accurately reflects the terms and conditions of the option we obtained.* I brought it here today from our normal files in which we keep all correspondence with our clients. Although I tried to acquire the necessary financing, we were short about $70,000 because the banks had a fifty percent capital requirement at

---

*The copy of the letter may be found on pp. 47-48.

that time. In addition, $80,000 would be necessary for new equipment purchases.

Oct. 2020

Mr. Rubino lost the entire South Elm Street plant to a fire on October 28, YR-2. Fortunately, the fire insurance coverage which was paid provided the additional capital. The insurance paid $300,000. The actual loss was $294,000, $20,000 of which went to customer claims for destroyed clothing. There was plenty of money left over for the warehouse and the equipment purchase. The fire was actually a godsend for Mr. Rubino. It really turned his business around.

godsend

(This deposition was taken in the office of defendant's counsel on October 7, YR-1. After it was transcribed, it was signed by the deponent, Edward George.)

Certified by:

Anne Dolan

ANNE DOLAN
Certified Shorthand Reporter (CSR)

Rubino Case File

DEPOSITION OF ANTHONY RUBINO*

ANTHONY RUBINO, called to testify on deposition by the plaintiff and having been duly sworn, testified as follows:

My name is Tony Rubino, and I am forty years old. I am married to the former Carol DiBartelemeo, and we have three children, Salvatore, age twelve, Mary, age nine, and Tony Jr., age four. We live in a house we bought in YR-3 at 3057 Nesper Street in the Northeast section of Nita City. We moved there from the old neighborhood in South Nita so the [handwritten: moved to Northillton] kids would have a better neighborhood to grow up in and have better schools to go to. The old neighborhood was fine when we were growing up, but it had changed a lot in the past few years, so we decided to move. The crime rate is way up, and the streets just aren't safe anymore. I graduated from high school in YR-20. I was never very good in school, and I flunked a couple times when I was in grade school. After graduation, I decided I should see some of the world, so I joined the Navy. I served on an aircraft carrier for four years and received an honorable discharge in YR-16. I thought about making the Navy a career, but my father wanted me to join the family business because I was his only son and because my four sisters were all married and busy raising kids. I remember when I got out of the Navy and returned home, there was a big party. My father took me down to the plant and unveiled the new sign on the front of the store, "Rubino and Son, Dry Cleaners." To this day he says that was the happiest day of his life.

I am now the manager and owner of the business. We have three retail stores and, since the fire, a new plant in the Northeast at 65100 Roosevelt Boulevard. My father started the business in YR-45. It started out as a laundry, but Pop worked really hard and expanded the place to include dry cleaning as well. About a year after I started working with him, he bought the building next to his on South Elm Street and expanded so he could do laundry for one of the local hospitals. The plant was located at 1050 South Elm Street. In YR-5, Pop had a heart attack, and the doctors told him he had to retire. It was pretty hard on him in the beginning, but he has adjusted to it now. In YR-4, when he finally

---

*The transcript of Rubino's deposition was excerpted so that only his answers are reprinted here. Assume that this is a true and accurate rendering of those answers. This deposition was taken in the office of plaintiff's counsel on October 18, YR-1.

accepted the fact that he was going to have to take it easy, he sold me the business for one dollar.

About that same time, I hired an accounting and business consulting firm, Bryant, George and White. Up until that time, Ray Rosen, who had been with my father since the very beginning, had done the books in addition to supervising the plant. But, I decided that it was time to modernize. Ed George came to the plant a number of times to review our books and our record keeping. We got one of those small computers for record keeping which I kept in my office at home. Also, we started to take credit cards. This was a big change for the business. In the old days, we did a complete cash-only business, and would always have $2,000 to $3,000 in the office safe at the South Elm Street plant. Ed George persuaded me that this was silly. At the time of the fire, we were keeping only a couple of hundred dollars at each of the retail outlets. This had been done for two years before the fire.

Also, Ed did some sort of study on the neighborhood. He advised me that the neighborhood was changing, and that it made good business sense to relocate. I told him that as long as my father was alive there would be a store on South Elm Street, but he did persuade me to open a number of retail stores in the Northeast. He said the Northeast was a much more stable area. Also, he advised me to get into the uniform business. It was a natural add-on to the dry cleaning and laundry business. What we did was to buy the uniforms custom made for our customers, and then rent them as well as clean them. It was a little shaky in the beginning, but after we got known in the community, business really picked up. We have several large accounts like the electric company and a car dealership and some smaller accounts like florists, gas stations, and small oil companies. We maintained the retail store on South Street, but the main reason for the building was to do all the cleaning.

By mid YR-2, it became apparent that it made no business sense to keep the plant and shop on South Elm Street. George pointed out that the retail business was off and also that we were wasting a lot of money on gas driving back and forth from the Northeast where our customers were to South Nita where the plant was. We started to investigate the possibility of buying a building in which we could relocate the plant and allow for expansion. George found a perfect building, close to our retail outlets and our uniform customers.

We had some problems, however, due to the economic situation in late YR-2 and early YR-1. The property we were interested in was on the market for $200,000. The banks

Another explanation of less cash

Wanted to keep South Store b/c dad

wanted us to put up fifty percent of the purchase price in order to finance the rest of the project. We also had projected that the cost of the new equipment would run an additional $80,000. George talked to the banks, and the best he could do was to get a guarantee for financing of $180,000 if we could put up $100,000 cash. Because we had expanded quickly during the three years before this, we didn't have that kind of capital. I was investigating alternative sources of capital during the first part of YR-1 because I was certain that the deal was the best we could get for years to come. We had an option on the property until March 1, YR-1, but I wasn't very confident we'd be able to go through on the deal. The letter you showed me is a copy of the letter I received in late September, YR-2. It sets out the terms of the deal on the Northeast property. The original was burned in the fire along with some other records.* Fortunately, most of the papers necessary to keep the business going were at my home.

On October 14, YR-2, another thing happened that made me want that deal even more. A group of militants went into Cohen's Department Store, just a few blocks away from our plant on South Elm Street, and shot up the place. A couple of people were killed--people from the neighborhood. A number of others were injured. There wasn't any reason for the shootings. It was known in the papers as the South Elm Street Massacre. I figured it was just a matter of time before it happened to us. I was real upset about the whole situation.

I remember talking to Bobby Delgreggo, a friend of mine and one of my employees, about the situation on a number of occasions. Bobby was a guy from the neighborhood who I grew up with. In fact, we graduated from high school together. After high school, while I was in the Navy, Bobby was in the Army. We both got out about the same time, but I didn't have much contact with him. In YR-3, Bobby came and asked me for a job. He told me that he'd had some trouble and was having a hard time finding work. He explained that three years before he had lost a lot of money to a number of bookies and that some tough guy had bought his markers. Bobby told me that to save his tail, he had agreed to torch a place to work off his debt. Bobby got caught and did time in prison for arson. Originally, I was a little nervous about hiring him. Because his father was a good friend of Pop and because he and I had been friends, I gave him a job as driver and mechanic. Bobby did real good work for me. In fact, he's now the supervisor at the new plant in the Northeast.

---

*The copy of the letter may be found on pp. 47-48.

I don't recall any specifics of the conversations we had. But I know that when I was real upset about the murders, Bobby offered to take care of business at the plant, you know, open up, take the receipts, just look after the place. He lived right by the South Elm Street plant. He kidded me about only needing $100,000 to open up the new plant, called me a big shot, and sometimes sort of reached in his pocket and offered to give me the money out of his loose change. I know that Ray Rosen says he overheard Bobby and me talking about setting fire to Pop's plant, but he's dead wrong. If he heard anything at all, he must have misunderstood. The plant sometimes got so noisy that you could hardly hear yourself think much less hear and remember a conversation you were eavesdropping on.

Like I said earlier, Ray Rosen worked for my father ever since I can remember. In fact, when we were kids, my sisters and I called him Uncle Ray. He did everything at the plant, from keeping the books and waiting on customers to repairing the equipment. Ray knew that I was thinking about moving the plant and was dead set against it. He also was mad at me because I refused to buy any new equipment for the South Elm Street plant. I'll have to admit that he did do a great job at keeping that old equipment running and making the old plant look as good as possible. About a month before the fire, Ray and Bobby painted the customer area. Now, I understand from the fire marshal that the drop cloths and paint rags from the painting, which were left in the storage room, probably caused the fire. I refused, however, to put any real money into the old plant because I wanted to open a new one. Also, the financial burden of opening the three new stores in the Northeast didn't leave a whole lot of money to put into the old equipment.

I know that Ray says he figured someone set the fire because the delivery trucks and most of the uniforms were out of the plant on the night of the fire, but that wasn't unusual. Every two weeks or so, we would load up the trucks and let our delivery people who lived in the Northeast drive the trucks home. Then, they could make deliveries when our customers opened at 6:30 a.m. If they had to come all the way to South Nita and then go all the way back up to the Northeast, the earliest delivery would be at 7:30 a.m. Most of our customers wanted their uniforms first thing in the morning. That's the reason that, even though the uniforms probably would have fit into two trucks, we used all three. That way, our best customers had the uniforms right at the beginning of their business day. It's this kind of service that keeps old customers and gets new ones.

The fire happened sometime during the early morning of October 28, YR-2. I got a call from the fire department at about 5:00 a.m., I called Bobby and Ray who lived closer, and then I went down to the plant. I got down to the plant a little after 6:00 a.m. and met Ray, Bobby, and Joe Ruggiero, the fire marshal. I knew Joe to say hello to because he was an old friend of my father. Joe told me that it looked like the fire started in the storeroom in the back and got out of control when the chemicals we used for dry cleaning exploded. He asked me if there was any reason I knew why someone would want to set fire to the plant. I told him no. Then he asked me if any of my employees had a criminal record, and I said something like, "Small potatoes." At that point, Bobby came up and Bobby and Ruggiero started talking. I really couldn't hear what they were saying. After that, Bobby walked over to me. He was real upset. I guess he blamed himself for the fire because of the rags and the drop cloths in the storage room. I told him not to worry about it, that he was a good worker, and that I'd take care of him. I don't know where Ray was at that time. Right after that, they pulled out the old safe. We opened it and found that it had protected the contents—some papers and about $300.00 in cash. The fire completely destroyed the plant and the small retail shop. Fortunately, the fire department kept it from spreading. We had to make good on all the clothes our customers had with us.

I had fire insurance with Nita Fire and Casualty Company through the Al Case Agency. The policy amount was $350,000. I went to see Al on the day of the fire. He told me he would file the claim with the home office as soon as he got my claim letter and Joe Ruggiero's report. The letter you showed me is the claim letter I sent to Al Case.* I admit that I padded the estimate by claiming loss of uniforms that were actually in the trucks, but that only amounted to about $6,000. I've already sent Al Case a check. The letter you showed me is the second letter I sent to Al Case. I did not, however, have anything to do with setting the fire, and I'm sure that Bobby didn't either. I'll admit that the fire was really a godsend. When the insurance paid off the full amount in early February, YR-1, I was able to go through on the deal in the Northeast. The letter and check you showed me are what I got from the insurance company. For the period from the fire until the new plant opened in May, YR-1, I was able to keep the stores open and to keep my uniform customers happy by subcontracting the cleaning business. That way, I didn't have to lay off most of my employees.

refunded for the false claim

---

*The correspondence between Case and Rubino and photocopies of the checks may be found on pages 49, 55 and 59.

After I completed the deal on the new plant, I talked with Ray about doing his old job at the new plant. I didn't really think he'd take it, but I felt I owed it to him because of his years with the business. He thought about it for a while and finally decided to retire a year early. My father always wanted Ray to be taken care of, so we gave him a good pension. Given what he's saying now, I'm not sure why we were so nice to him.

When Ray turned down the job as plant supervisor, I decided to offer the job to Bobby. Although this meant raising Bobby's salary from about $11,000 to $15,000, I was still making out because Ray's salary was $21,000 when he retired. I know that Bobby bought a new Cadillac, cash money, in February, YR-1. I still kid him about driving a better car than the boss and ask whether he robbed a bank to get the money. Actually, Bobby hit it big at the casinos in Atlantic City and decided to spend the money before he lost it. He certainly could not have afforded that car on what I pay him.

I have looked at the diagram* you showed me and it is accurate. The building had oil heat in every room but the storage room and garage where we used space heaters when necessary.

(This deposition was taken in the office of plaintiff's counsel on October 18, YR-1. After it was transcribed, it was signed by the deponent, Anthony Rubino.)

Certified by:

Paula J. Brooks

PAULA J. BROOKS
Certified Shorthand Reporter (CSR)

---

* See p. 45.

DEPOSITION OF ROBERT DELGREGGO*

ROBERT DELGREGGO, called to testify on deposition by the plaintiff and having been duly sworn, testified as follows:

My name is Robert Delgreggo, but I go by Bobby. I am thirty-eight years old and now live in an apartment at 1500 Academy Road in the Northeast. At the time of the fire, I lived in the third floor apartment of my parents' house on Christian Street in South Nita. My parents' house is about four blocks from the old Rubino and Son plant which was at 1050 South Elm Street. At the time of the fire, I was employed by Rubino's as a delivery driver and part-time mechanic. Now, I'm a supervisor at the new plant. My boss, Tony Rubino, is a friend of mine from the neighborhood. He is two years older than I, but we graduated from high school together because he was kept back a couple of times when he was a kid. After graduation from high school in YR-20 I went into the Army. I served for four years. I was always interested in cars when I was growing up. While in the Army, I worked in a motor pool, I was trained as a mechanic, and I drove small transport trucks. I received an honorable discharge in YR-16 and returned home to Nita City. I worked fairly steady for a number of small trucking firms, driving short hauls and working as a part-time mechanic.

I've always had a weakness for gambling, and I guess you'd say this was my downfall. I was arrested and con-victed for gambling a number of times between YR-14 and YR-6. In YR-6, I got in serious money trouble with a number of bookies. They put a lot of pressure on me to pay some gambling debts. The debts amounted to about $6,000, but I didn't have the money. I was approached by a bookie who had bought all my markers. He told me I could work off the whole debt in one night by setting fire to an abandoned building. He promised me that no one would be in the building, so I agreed to do it. I guess it was for the insurance. I really don't think I had much choice; it was the building or me. Anyhow, I got caught, charged, and con-victed of arson in YR-6. I could have gotten off for no jail time if I was willing to testify against the guy who had my markers, but I figured prison was better than dealing

Not his choice to set fire [handwritten margin note]

---

*The transcript of Delgreggo's deposition was excerpted so that only his answers are reprinted here. Assume that this is a true and accurate rendering of those answers. This deposition was taken in the office of plaintiff's coun-sel on October 18, YR-1.

with him. I was sentenced to two to five years in the Nita Penitentiary. I was paroled in June, YR-3. I have been shown a copy of my arrest and conviction record and, to the best of my knowledge, it is accurate.*

After I got out of prison, I returned to the neighborhood in Nita City. While I was in prison, I heard that Mr. Rubino, Tony's father, had a heart attack and was forced to retire. He and my father had been friends and, as I said, so were Tony and myself. After running into a lot of people who wouldn't hire me because of my record, I asked Tony for a job. He had been working for his father since getting out of the Navy and actually took over the business in YR-4 when his father got sick. Tony hired me to work as a delivery truck driver. I also did minor repairs and maintenance on the delivery trucks.

Even though Tony had never been real smart in school, he had turned into a pretty good businessman. He turned what had been a neighborhood cleaners into a pretty good business and had opened three retail stores in the Northeast. He also had gotten into the uniform rental business and, from what I could tell, was making real good money. He moved his family up to the Northeast when he opened up the stores there. He told me that he didn't like what was happening to the neighborhood, and he wanted his kids to have a better place to grow up and go to school. Because I was single I really didn't mind the old neighborhood, but it had gotten pretty tough. I could understand why Tony didn't want to raise his kids there.

My job at Rubino's in YR-2 was to pick up and make deliveries at the businesses that used the uniform service and make minor repairs on the delivery trucks. I worked from about 6:00 a.m. to 3:30 or 4:00 p.m. Our customers--car dealerships, oil companies, gas stations, and the electric company--were located in the Northeast. The trucks were normally garaged at the South Street plant. They were loaded there and then driven to make deliveries of the uniforms. This was also where I did the repair work. We kept tools, oil, and parts in the storage area next to the garage. I have looked at the diagram of the South Street plant, and it looks accurate to me.

In October of YR-2, a horrible murder took place at Cohen's Department Store, which was about three blocks from Rubino's on South Elm Street. A bunch of guys went into the store and ended up shooting up the place, killing two people

---

*The copy of Delgreggo's record may be found on p. 61.

and hurting some others. There didn't seem to be any reason for it; they weren't even robbing the place. The papers say it was some kind of militant group that thought Cohen's was ripping off their people, but I don't know anything about that. I do know that Tony was real upset by the whole thing. It seemed like that was all he could talk about from the time of the killing until the fire, two weeks later. I remember sitting in his office at the plant and talking about it with him. He kept saying that he had to get out, that the neighborhood had changed, and that it was just too crazy for him. I remember during one conversation he said that he just had to get out of the South Elm Street plant. I remember telling him I would take care of the plant, you know, opening and closing. Tony told me he would think about it. About the same time, Tony told me that he had a chance to relocate the main plant in the Northeast, but he was having trouble getting the up-front money together. I remember joking with him that it was no problem, that I'd just write him a check.

What Ray overheard

On October 28, YR-2, there was a fire at the South Street plant. I got a call from Tony at about 5:00 a.m. and went right over to the plant where I met a guy from the fire department. I think his name was Ruggiero, but I can't be sure. He somehow knew about my record for arson and asked where I had been that night. I told him I went to bed about 10:30 p.m. because work started early. Then, he asked me what we kept in the storage room, and I told him about the oil, rags, tools, etc. I also told him there were some drop cloths and rags left over from when Ray Rosen and I painted the customer area about a month before the fire. I know the painting stuff was there because Ray wasn't feeling well and I cleaned up by myself. Then he went to talk to some of the firemen, and I waited around for Tony to get there.

Ray wasn't sure about drop cloths

After Tony arrived, the guy from the fire department, who Tony called Joe, came over to us and said the fire started in the storage area. I realized that the fire was probably my fault for not keeping the storage area clean. I felt real bad because of this. I apoligized to Tony about five times. He was real good about it, and he said that I always did good work for him and that as far as he was concerned I had a job with him for life. I know that Ray Rosen says that I started the fire so Tony could get the insurance money, but that's just not true. I think Ray's just upset because Tony decided to buy the new plant in the Northeast. Because Ray didn't want to make the commute, he retired. I really don't know what his problem was. Tony and his dad gave Ray a real good pension. He gets Social Security, too. Anyway, he had to be sixty-five or seventy when the fire happened so he should have been happy to retire. I know Ray

Bobby upset

Says Ray's upset

thinks that it's important that the trucks and a bunch of uniforms had been taken out of the plant on the day of the fire, but that wasn't unusual. Sometimes, maybe once a month, when we had to make real early deliveries, we loaded the trucks the night before and the drivers who lived in the Northeast would take them home and make the deliveries in the morning. Like I said, all of our uniform business was in that part of the city, and it's a good forty-five minute drive one way from the Northeast to the South Street plant.

It's true that I bought a Cadillac for $15,000 cash in February of YR-1. Like I said, gambling had always been a weakness for me. I had gone to Atlantic City for the weekend, and got real hot. Rather than losing everything I won, I decided to buy the car I'd always wanted.

After Tony bought the new plant, I moved to the Northeast so I could be near my work. The apartment is a little more expensive, $300 per month as opposed to $195 per month. But when Ray retired, Tony gave me the job as supervisor for the new plant and I got a raise from $11,500 per year to $15,000 per year. Tony told me that if I keep up the good work, I could expect a nice raise. This is important because I've recently decided to get married. My fiancee, Julie, works now, but we'd like to start a family real soon.

That's everything I can remember about the fire.

(This deposition was taken in the office of plaintiff's counsel on October 18, YR-1. After it was transcribed, it was signed by the deponent, Robert Delgreggo.)

Certified by:

Paula J. Brooks

PAULA J. BROOKS
Certified Shorthand Reporter (CSR)

Bought Car gambling

investigator for insurance

DEPOSITION OF BRYCE STENTON PUGH*

BRYCE STENTON PUGH, called to testify on deposition by the defendant and having been duly sworn, testified as follows:

My name is Bryce Stenton Pugh, and my office is located in Hartford, Connecticut. I am an independent contractor specializing in the investigation and determination of cause in industrial fires. I am on retainer with a number of insurance companies, and I testify frequently as an expert witness in civil cases concerning the cause and origin of fires. My annual income from this business is approximately $120,000.00.

I was employed by the Nita Fire and Casualty Company to investigate the fire at Rubino and Son, Dry Cleaners, 1050 South Elm Street, Nita City, Nita, which occurred on October 28, YR-2. The company has paid the claim on this fire in the amount of $300,000. It is unusual to be employed after payment on the policy, but it is by no means uncommon. My $8,000 annual retainer with this company covers the cost of my investigation of this and other fires, as well as my fee for this deposition. Should I have to testify at trial, my fee will be an additional $5,000 plus expenses. There is no contingent fee or bonus.

I received a bachelor of science degree in chemistry from Nita University in YR-22 and a master of science degree in chemistry from Nita State University in YR-20. Then I entered the Air Force, and I served for five years. I specialized in fire detection and control. My training in the Air Force included chemistry courses specifically related to fire control and detection. I received an honorable discharge with the rank of captain in YR-15. Then, I went to Cal Tech where I received my Ph.D. in criminology in YR-12.

I am a member of the National Council of Fire Examiners. I was accepted into the council after completing a comprehensive written and oral examination in YR-12. Membership in the council represents certification of expertise in much

_____

*The transcript of Pugh's deposition was excerpted so that only his answers are reprinted here. Assume that this is a true and accurate rendering of those answers. This deposition was taken in the office of defendant's counsel on October 8, YR-1.

the same way as being board certified in the medical profession. I have written widely in this field. Some of my articles are "Legal Aspects of Arson," "Convicting the Arsonists," "Tips for the Arson Investigator," "Understanding the Corpus Delicti Rule," and "Defining 'Incendiary Origin.'" These articles have appeared in publications such as the <u>Journal of Criminal Law and Science</u>, the <u>American Criminal Law Review</u>, the <u>Journal of Insurance Underwriters</u>, and the <u>Nita Law Review</u>.

I have testified in over one hundred civil cases and in about a dozen criminal cases. I have always testified on behalf of insurance companies or the prosecution. Yes, I have always testified that a fire was incendiary in origin. Those cases in which my opinion was that the fire was accidental in nature were settled by the insurance companies.

I have no doubt that the Rubino fire was incendiary in origin, that is, it was set by a human being. There was no accidental source. I arrived at this conclusion because there were three separate points of origin for the fire. It is a basic opinion, found in all the literature, that multiple points of origin indicate arson.

I did not physically inspect the premises, but I studied the reports and talked to the fire marshal. There were three separate non-communicating fires. The civilian, John Andrews, saw a fire in the clothing area. Then, purely by coincidence, he saw the explosion in the dry cleaning area.

Spontaneous combustion is extremely rare. There is no proof that only paint-soaked rags were in the storage room. Ray Rosen conceded that some of the facility had been painted about a month before the fire, and that the rags could have been in the room, but he did not see them.

The storage room was not insulated well enough to create the kind of condition required to preserve enough heat for spontaneous combustion.

Motor oil with hydrocarbon will not cause spontaneous combustion. However, the oil in paint dries and hardens by oxidation at the double covalent bonds. This generates heat if there is sufficient insulation.

My questioning of Rosen showed that the storage room was cold and unheated. This is confirmed by Rubino's statement to the fire marshal. There was no radiator in the room, and the small window was not a storm window. During the day, with the dryer and pressers going, the room was not cold. But at night, the room would be quite cold. Under these conditions, spontaneous ignition or combustion would not occur. This assumes the presence of sufficiently oily rags and drop cloths. While the fireball could travel as Ruggiero suggests, it is just as likely that the fire would hit the clothes and clothing bags first. These would ignite first, and there would not have been an explosion until the entire building had been engulfed.

Other information from Ray Rosen and Edward George corroborates the physical evidence. I have reviewed their depositions. Anthony Rubino and Bobby Delgreggo have refused to talk with me. At the time of the fire, three delivery trucks and virtually all the uniforms owned by the business, which were normally garaged at the building, had been moved. Mr. Rosen had overheard several conversations, a fair interpretation of which would be that Mr. Rubino and Mr. Delgreggo planned to burn the building. The laundry was in financial difficulty at the time of the fire. Also, there was substantially less money in the store safe than was normally kept on hand.

What he based conclusions on — all have explanations

Based on all of the above, I have no doubt as to the incendiary origin of this fire.

(This deposition was taken in the office of defendant's counsel on October 8, YR-1. After it was transcribed, it was signed by the deponent, Bryce Stenton Pugh.)

Certified by:

Anne Dolan

ANNE DOLAN
Certified Shorthand Reporter (CSR)

DEPOSITION OF JOSEPH RUGGIERO*

JOSEPH RUGGIERO, called to testify on deposition by the plaintiff and having been duly sworn, testified as follows:

My name is Joseph Ruggiero and I am fifty-five years old. I am married and have three grown children, all of whom live in Nita City. I am employed by the Nita City Fire Department as a fire marshal and have held that position for sixteen years.

I received my first training in fire fighting while I was in the Navy from YR-38 through YR-35. During that time, I was a fireman on a destroyer. In YR-35, I received an honorable discharge from the Navy and went to work as a fireman in Nita City. I worked my way up through the ranks and in YR-23, after scoring well on the civil service test (I was in the top twenty-five), I became a chief in one of the districts. I held that position until YR-16 when I again scored well on the civil service test and became a fire marshal. For the past seven years, I have been in charge of training for newly appointed fire marshals. In addition to my Navy training and my years of experience, I have taken courses in fire prevention and control at Nita Community College. I have also attended many seminars, the most recent being a seven-day course in Washington, D.C. in YR-3. It was offered by the Justice Department and was entitled "Detecting Arson for Hire." I have testified as an expert witness in over 200 trials in the Nita courts. Most of these appearances have been in criminal cases, but I occasionally testify in civil matters.

I know the Rubino family. I have known Salvatore Rubino since we were kids in South Nita. We played ball together and I think he still belongs to the same Sons of Italy Lodge, but I haven't seen him since his heart attack a few years back. I know Anthony, but not very well. He's a hard working kid with some business sense.

On October 28, YR-2, I was on duty from midnight to eight a.m. Two fire marshals are always on duty around the clock. I was assigned to the Rubino fire by my chief, Commander Gillespie.

---

*The transcript of Ruggiero's deposition was excerpted so that only his answers are reprinted here. Assume that this is a true and accurate rendering of those answers. This deposition was taken in the office of plaintiff's counsel on October 19, YR-1.

I got to the premises at about 5:00 a.m. and talked to several firemen. I also talked to the citizen, John Andrews, who turned in the alarm. When I arrived, the fire was still smoldering, and I was unable to enter the building until about 5:45 a.m.

I conducted a physical inspection of the premises. I located the source of the fire, or the low point of the burn, on the southwest wall of the building. There was a small room in the building that was used to store equipment and spare parts for the delivery trucks, which were normally parked in the garage in the rear of the plant. Motor oil and machine oil were also kept in this room since Rubino's serviced its own trucks. In addition, there were some drop cloths from a recent paint job.

The fire started through spontaneous combustion when the rags ignited. The wall was just a wallboard, and the fire rapidly burned through it to an area used to store clothing. The fire gained momentum, and then leaped about sixty-five feet to the northwest wall where dry cleaning chemicals were kept in an uncovered alcove. These chemicals were naptha or napthene, which are commonly found in dry cleaning establishments. They were stored in ten pound jugs. A loose cap and some spillage undoubtedly aided the crossover. I can't positively say that there was a loose cap or spillage, but this is inevitable in even the neatest establishment.

Once the dry cleaning chemicals ignited, there was an explosion. It is possible that the fire also leaped to clothing on the north side of the store near the front window. But, since the clothing was consumed, I can't say for sure.

The wooden floor under the rags and oil was burned completely through. The floor, composed of southern pine, was decaying. This material burns at a relatively low temperature, about 300° F. For example, chemically fireproofed wood will not burn until 1200° F. This is the only spot where the floor burned completely through. This was very important in my findings because it indicates that the fire burned there the longest time.

Even under the cleaning fluids and chemicals, a very hot point, the floor was not completely burned through. It was burned down about two inches, indicating an explosion. The floor in between was only slightly burned--about one inch.

The front windows were blown out by the explosion. It was a very cold and windy night. After the windows went, the gusty winds aided the rapid burning process.

Source of Fire

Rubino Case File

The ceiling on the building was completely destroyed. The ceiling is about fifteen feet high. The fire burned upwards to the highest point. This is consistent with the open nature of the plant. There were no retaining walls or fire doors. The south wall was heavily damaged and destroyed at the point of origin.

It is ludicrous to suggest that there were three separate fires. Nearly every fire is going to burn unevenly. I can explain easily the leap of sixty-five feet. The fire in the enclosed area burned up all the oxygen and a fireball was created because any fire seeks air. This search for air causes the leaping phenomenon commonly known as flashover. The fire sought its way into the open area. The hottest point between the enclosed area and the open area was at the location of the chemicals. It is also possible that the fire jumped to the clothing at the same time.

Anyone who says it was arson has to explain these three fires. It would be very easy to light a fire in the clothing, probably with an open flame. Yes, this would burn slowly at first. But by the same token, it would be very dangerous to light these chemicals by an open flame and then get out of there before an explosion. It would be very risky--not impossible, I'm not saying that.

It also would be possible to light a fire in the storage room by the application of an open flame. But then I think the pattern would have been different. The floor under the storage area would not have burned completely through.

I saw Mr. Delgreggo at about 5:15 a.m. I also saw Ray Rosen and Tony. Tony arrived later than the other two. They were all very upset. Tony just stood there quietly. Ray was crying softly, and Bobby just kept saying, "My God."

Later that day, Tony and I talked in my office. I asked him a routine list of questions about who locked up and so on.

I didn't suspect arson. I did not <u>not</u> suspect arson either. I had an open mind.

I did ask about criminal records and Tony said something which indicated nothing major. I cannot recall if I specifically mentioned arson. I may have. I knew Delgreggo and I knew he'd done some time, but I did not know what for. I just was not thinking about it when I talked to Tony.

I don't remember exactly when I heard about Delgreggo's conviction for arson. I did not, however, learn about it before I concluded that the fire was accidental in origin. It does not change my opinion at all.

I did not know the trucks had been loaded with uniforms and moved. That doesn't change my opinion either.

I was not aware of the financial condition of the company or its plans and difficulties. Sure, it is something I should have considered, but how was I to know? Yes, I was aware of the murder at Cohens, everyone was, but no one else burned their business.

On February 15, YR-1, Ray Rosen came into my office complaining that the fire had been set by Delgreggo. I tried to be nice to him but finally had to ask him to leave, saying that I knew my business and to take it easy. I haven't talked to anyone from Rubino's since the morning of the fire, except Rosen.

The report that I prepared in the weeks after the fire was provided to Mr. Pugh from the Nita Fire and Casualty Company.* I also had a conversation with Pugh and told him just what I've told you today. I am still convinced that the fire was not the result of arson.

(This deposition was taken in the office of plaintiff's counsel on October 19, YR-1. After it was transcribed, it was signed by the deponent, Joseph Ruggiero.)

Certified by:

Paula J. Brooks

PAULA J. BROOKS
Certified Shorthand Reporter
(CSR)

---

*A copy of Ruggiero's report may be found on p. 63.

C. EXHIBITS

Rubino Case File

Nita City Inquirer

afternoon edition, October 28, YR-2

Fire Destroys Nita City Landmark

by Linda Sommin, Staff Reporter

An early morning fire completely destroyed the South Nita City landmark of Rubino and Son, Dry Cleaners today.

No one was injured, but Fire Marshal Joseph Ruggiero described the damage as a total loss.

The fire was discovered by John Andrews of Nita City who summoned the fire department at 4:08 a.m. Firefighters were unable to stop the fire from moving rapidly through the wood frame and stucco-covered building, although they did keep it from spreading to adjoining buildings. The blaze was declared under control within an hour.

Fire Marshal Ruggiero stated that the fire apparently was caused by spontaneous combustion in a storage room located in the back of the premises. Foul play is not suspected.

Rubino and Son, established by Salvatore Rubino in YR-45, has served South Nita City at 1050 South Elm Street continuously since that date. It currently is owned and operated by the founder's son, Anthony Rubino. The younger Rubino, who was called to the scene, declined comment when asked if the business would reopen.

SOUTH ELM STREET

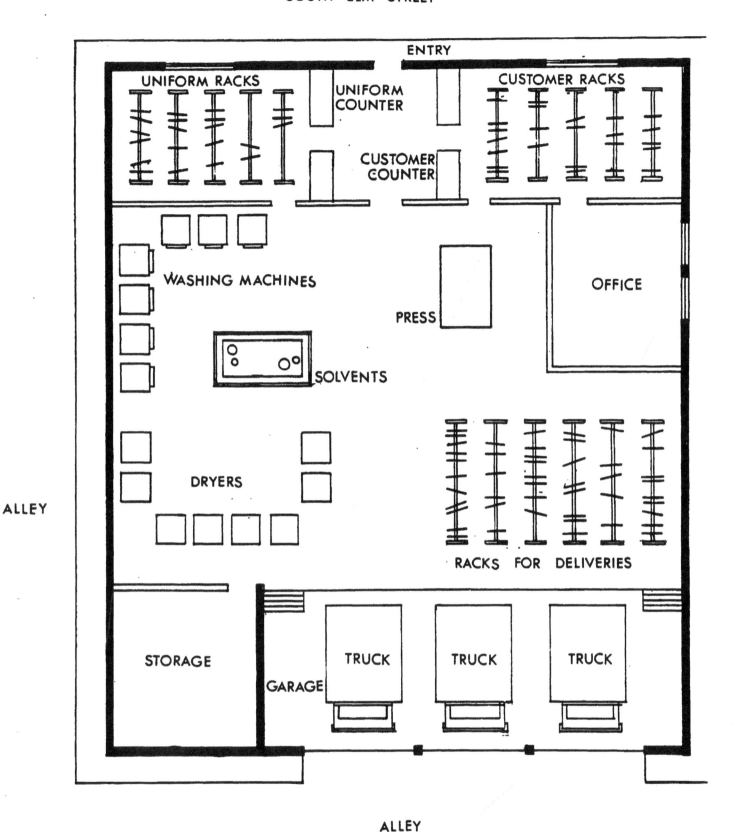

ENTRY

UNIFORM RACKS

UNIFORM COUNTER

CUSTOMER RACKS

CUSTOMER COUNTER

WASHING MACHINES

PRESS

OFFICE

SOLVENTS

DRYERS

RACKS FOR DELIVERIES

STORAGE

GARAGE

TRUCK　　TRUCK　　TRUCK

ALLEY

ALLEY

FLOOR DIAGRAM
Rubino & Son, Dry Cleaners
1050 South Elm Street

LEGEND
Inside walls are 7 feet high. Open space between top of walls and ceiling.

N

Rubino Case File

Exhibit 3

BRYANT, GEORGE AND WHITE

Certified Public Accountants
Business Consultants
1410 Main Street
Nita City, Nita

September 25, YR-2

Mr. Anthony Rubino
Rubino and Son, Dry Cleaners
1050 South Elm Street
Nita City, Nita

Dear Tony:

This is to confirm our phone conversation of this afternoon concerning the potential purchase of the warehouse at 65100 Roosevelt Boulevard in Northeast, Nita City.

As we discussed, the property in question is available for the price of $200,000.00. I have investigated the property and have found that it is well worth the asking price. It will provide space for all foreseeable expansion. From the information I've been able to gather, the equipment necessary to open operations at this location would require an additional minimum investment of of $80,000.00.

Looking toward this potential purchase, I have made inquiries into financing with the banking community. Unfortunately, given current economic conditions, they will want a capital investment of at least $100,000.00 before financing the rest of the deal. After reviewing the books for your business, the most we could squeeze out at this time is about $30,000.00 cash.

Therefore, I suggest that you investigate other sources of capital. Although time is short, you may be able to find a buyer for the South Elm Street property. I have acquired, for the amount of $5,000.00, an option on the Roosevelt Boulevard property as you requested. The option extends until March 1, YR-1.

Mr. Anthony Rubino
September 25, YR-2
Page Two

If you need any further information, or if you can
obtain the necessary capital, call me immediately. As I've
said, this represents an excellent opportunity to guarantee
the continued growth of your business.

Sincerely,

Edward George

EDWARD GEORGE
C.P.A.

Exhibit 4

RUBINO AND SON, DRY CLEANERS
1050 South Elm Street
Nita City, Nita

November 5, YR-2

Mr. Albert Case
Nita Fire and Casualty Company
403 South Alder Street
Nita City, Nita

Dear Al:

Attached is the itemized claim form for damages as the result of the fire of October 28, YR-2. I'm not sure what we'll do about the plant on South Elm Street, but this may be one of the last times I use this stationery. Pop is taking the fire a lot better than I thought. I know he appreciated your call.

Looking forward to hearing from you.

Sincerely,

Anthony J Rubino

Anthony J. Rubino

AJR/ns
enc.

Exhibit 5

NITA FIRE AND CASUALTY COMPANY

STATEMENT OF LOSS

Policy Holder: Rubino and Son, Dry Cleaners

Policy No. BF-24-076-1112-5

Policy Limit: $350,000

Date of Loss: October 28, YR-2

ITEMS OF LOSS	VALUE
1. Building	$238,000.00
2. Equipment	35,000.00
3. Materials	450.00
4. Supplies	550.00
5. Uniforms	6,000.00
6. Customer Cleaning	20,000.00
7. ----------------	--------
8. ----------------	--------
9. ----------------	--------
10. ----------------	--------
TOTAL VALUE	$300,000.00

Anthony J Rubino
Claimant

Subscribed and sworn to before me this 5th day of November, YR-2.

Nancy Sanford
Notary Public

Exhibit 6

NITA
FIRE AND CASUALTY
COMPANY

Number One
Charter Oak Plaza
Nita City, Nita
06492

February 1, YR-1

Mr. Anthony J. Rubino
1050 South Elm Street
Nita City, Nita

RE: POLICY NO. BF-24-076-1112-5

Dear Mr. Rubino:

After consulting with our adjuster, we are pleased to remit to you this check in the amount of $300,000.00.

The loss by fire is always a tragic event. Fortunately, you had the foresight to insure with Nita Fire and Casualty.

We stand by you.

Sincerely,

Phillip Thereault
President

PT/jd

Nita Fire and Casualty Company
Nita City, Nita

February 1, YR-1

280

PAY TO THE
ORDER OF   Anthony J. Rubino, Rubino & Son, Dry Cleaners $ 300,000.00

Three Hundred Thousand and 00/100 ————————————————— Dollars

NITA NATIONAL BANK
Nita City, Nita

PRESIDENT

⑈080280⑈ ⑈031008003⑈ 2⑈615 300⑈

This check is endorsed on the back by Anthony J. Rubino
to Account Number 0-685-461, Nita National Bank, which is
the account of Rubino and Son, Dry Cleaners.

Exhibit 8

RUBINO AND SON, DRY CLEANERS
65100 Roosevelt Boulevard
Nita City, Nita

February 15, YR-1

Mr. Albert Case
Nita Fire and Casualty
Company
403 South Alder Street
Nita City, Nita

Dear Al:

First, thank you for processing our claim so quickly.
As you can see from the letterhead, we've decided to move
the operation up to the Northeast. Even though we won't
actually open until this fall, I'm confident that it's a
good move for the business.

The other reason I'm writing is to correct an error I
made when filing the claim for the fire. In the confusion
after the fire, I put in for $6,000 for uniforms I thought
we had lost. Actually, we didn't lose those uniforms, so
I'm enclosing a check for $6,090 which represents the amount
paid plus 1½% interest for the full month of February, 1981.
Sorry for any inconvenience.

Sincerely,

ANTHONY J. RUBINO

AJR/ns
ENCLOSURE

Rubino Case File

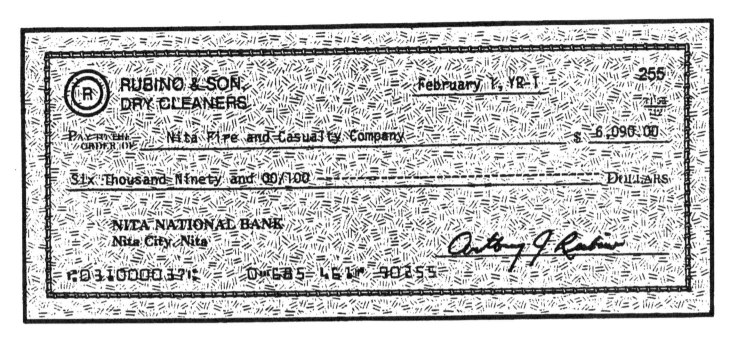

This check is stamped on the back: "FOR DEPOSIT ONLY, NITA FIRE AND CASUALTY COMPANY, Account Number 2-615-300, Nita National Bank."

Exhibit 10

UNIFORM ARREST AND DISPOSITION RECORD

Name: Robert Delgreggo	D.O.B. June 4, YR-38
S.S. No. 102-47-9203	P.O.B. Nita City, Nita

DATE	ADDRESS	OFFENSE	DISPOSITION
1/25/YR-14	1024 Christian St. Nita City, Nita	Gambling	Dismissed with Leave
4/15/YR-13	1024 Christian St. Nita City, Nita	Gambling	Guilty Plea 6 mo. probation
11/11/YR-12	1024 Christian St. Nita City, Nita	Gambling	Guilty Plea $25.00 fine
10/6/YR-11	1024 Christian St. Nita City, Nita	Gambling	Dismissed with Leave
8/31/YR-10	1024 Christian St. Nita City, Nita	Assault (misdemeanor)	Guilty Plea $50.00 fine
12/5/YR-10	1024 Christian St. Nita City, Nita	Gambling	Dismissed with Leave
6/14/YR-8	1024 Christian St. Nita City, Nita	Gambling	Guilty Plea $50.00 fine
9-11-YR-7	1024 Christian St. Nita City, Nita	Gambling	Guilty Plea 6 mos. suspended
5-10-YR-6	1024 Christian St. Nita City, Nita	Arson (felony)	Guilty Plea 2-5 years
			Paroled 6/4/YR-3

Certified as of 8/1/YR-1

Alexander McConachie   *Garrett D. Witte*

Alexander McConachie   Notary Public
Superintendant of Documents

Rubino Case File

Rubino Case File

Exhibit 11

INVESTIGATIVE REPORT

RUBINO AND SON, DRY CLEANERS

10/28/YR-2

Time of Alarm

Nita Hook and Ladder No. 3 responded to a box at 4:03 a.m. on 10/28/YR-2. The alarm was turned in by a passerby, John Andrews, Nita. A second company, No. 7, was called at 4:28 a.m.

Fire Dept. Response

Lt. Hertel, first on the scene with No. 3, reported that flames were raging through the front windows, which had been blown out. Flames also were coming from the ceiling. Hoses were used atop 1052 South Elm Street, a four story structure. Flames were raging from rear of premises as well.

No. 7 was called to assist because of concern about adjacent properties.

Fireman Montgomery went immediately to rear of premises. Flames were deep red with a small amount of smoke.

Fireman Jenkins operated hoses from 1052. Roof collapsed about 4:55 a.m. This aided flow of water into premises.

Description of Premises

The site is a wood frame and stucco structure. It fronts on the south of South Elm Street. It is eighty feet wide and one hundred feet deep. It is a story and a half with a ceiling about fifteen feet. The northeast side was used for customer service and the short-term storage of laundry and dry cleaning. To the west is the dry cleaning area with washers, pressers, dryers, and cleaning solvents.

To the rear, on the east side, is a small storage area and garage, which opens into the dry cleaning area. There is a driveway on the west side leading to South Elm Street. The garage is about twenty feet deep and about seventy feet in width and occupies all but ten feet on either side of the premises.

Origin of the Fire

The low burn was located in the rear of the premises on the west side. There is a 10 x 10 storage room, which was used to hold motor oil, tools, and other items used to service the trucks. The burn began at floor level, and the floor was burned completely through. The premises had been painted within the last month and oily rags were said to be stored in the room.

A hydrocarbon detector was used at about 5:30 a.m. to determine the presence of accelerants. Test was negative.

The pattern of the fire was upward to the ceiling and through a dry wall partition. The fire jumped to a small open storage area in the dry cleaning section. The chemicals and cleaning solvents with naptha base were stored in several ten gallon jugs in this area. This caused an explosion. The fire again burned upward to the ceiling. Much of the floor and walls between the two points was not destroyed. Burning in the floor (6" pine) was only about two inches.

Clothing stored in the northeast corner was completely destroyed. Floor was burned more deeply in this spot. Ceiling may have fallen into this area.

Electrical wiring was eliminated as a cause.

Interviews

1. John Andrews, 220 South Elm Street, was on his way to work at about 4:00 a.m. He was stopped at the light near 11th Street. His attention was attracted to the laundry facility by a red glow in the front window which he could see from his automobile. This was on the northeast wall of the store. There was then a loud explosion in the dry cleaning area on the west side of the store. Andrews then drove to 12th Street where he pulled an alarm and called 911.

2. Anthony Rubino, 3057 Nesper Street, owner and operator of involved premises. States no known reason for fire to start, no enemies, no disgruntled employees, no employees with significant criminal records. Reports that premises

was dry cleaning and laundry establishment, about 8,000 square feet, wood frame, stucco structure, open, with office, customer area, work area, garage (unheated) and storage room (unheated), pine floors throughout. Solvents for use in dry cleaning are stored in work area. Oily rags, painting rags and drop cloths, tools, and oil stored in storage room. Owner estimates total loss, approximates damage at $250,000-$300,000. Building was insured with Nita Fire and Casualty Company.

3.   Robert Delgreggo, 1024 Christian Street, employee at Rubino Laundry. Arrived at scene at approximately 5:20 a.m. Confirms presence of painting rags and drop cloths in storage room. Was asleep when called by A. Rubino to come to site of fire.

4.   Raymond Rosen, 1225 Catherine Street, supervisor, plant manager at Rubino laundry. Seemed quite agitated, but confirms contents of storage room. Couldn't get any other information.

D. PROPOSED JURY INSTRUCTIONS.*

1. The court will now instruct you as to the law to apply to the facts as you find them. You must apply the law as I instruct you, not as you think it might be or should be. This is important so that every citizen making a claim or defense will be treated equally under the law.

2. The parties to this case are Nita Fire and Casualty Company, the plaintiff, and Anthony J. Rubino, doing business as Rubino and Son, Dry Cleaners, the defendant. The parties have agreed to, and you must regard as conclusively proven, the following facts:

a. The plaintiff issued a fire insurance policy to the defendant on March 1, YR-2, covering loss due to fire at the insured premises located at 1050 South Elm Street, Nita City, Nita.

b. The insurance policy was in effect on October 28, YR-2.

c. On October 28, YR-2, the insurance policy covered all losses, up to and including $350,000, due to fire at the insured premises.

d. On October 28, YR-2, a fire destroyed the defendant's insured premises located at 1050 South Elm Street, Nita City, Nita, causing damages in the amount of $296,000.00.

e. The plaintiff has paid the defendant the total amount of loss, $294,000.00.

3. The plaintiff now claims that the fire on October 28, YR-2, at the defendant's premises at 1050 South Elm Street, Nita City, Nita, was a result of the intentional actions of the defendant or one acting in concert with the defendant.

4. The plaintiff has the burden of proving by a preponderance of the evidence that the fire on October 28, YR-2, at the defendant's premises at 1050 South Elm Street, Nita City, Nita, was the result of the intentional actions of the defendant or one acting in concert with the defendant.

---

* These proposed jury instructions are applicable to this case only. They may be used in conjunction with general jury instructions.

5. A preponderance of the evidence means evidence that, when weighed against that opposed to it, has more convincing force and the greater probability of truth. In the event that the evidence is evenly balanced so that you are unable to say that the evidence on either side of an issue preponderates, then your finding upon that issue must be against the party who had the burden of proving it.

6. In determining whether an issue has been proven by a preponderance of the evidence, you should consider all of the evidence bearing upon that issue regardless of who produced it.

7. Should you find that the plaintiff has proved by a preponderance of the evidence that the fire on October 28, YR-2, at the defendant's premises at 1050 South Elm Street, Nita City, Nita, was the result of the intentional actions of the defendant or one acting in concert with the defendant, then you should enter a verdict for the plaintiff. However, should you find that the plaintiff has failed to meet its burden by a preponderance of the evidence, then you should find for the defendant.

E. FORM OF VERDICT

IN THE CIRCUIT COURT OF
DARROW COUNTY, NITA
CIVIL DIVISION

NITA FIRE AND CASUALTY COMPANY,)
)
                    Plaintiff,)
)
          v.   )
)   JURY VERDICT
ANTHONY J. RUBINO, D.B.A.   )
RUBINO AND SON, DRY CLEANERS,   )
)
                    Defendant.   )

We, the jury, return the following verdict and each of us con-
curs in this verdict:

(Choose the appropriate verdict.)

I.

We, the jury, find for the plaintiff in the sum of

$_____.

_____
Foreperson

II.

We, the jury find for the defendant.

_____
Foreperson